FINDING FREEDOM FROM CLUTTER

TOP TIPS AND TRICKS FROM A PERSONAL
CONCIERGE AND CERTIFIED PHOTO MANAGER
TO GET RID OF CLUTTER AND ORGANIZE YOUR
PHOTOS, HOME, AND LIFE

MELISSA DRAVING

Internet addresses given in this book were accurate at the time it went to press.

Printed in the United States of America

Published in Hellertown, PA

Cover design by Katelyn Kozlowski

Library of Congress Control Number 2023910364

ISBN 978-1-958711-55-2

2 4 6 8 10 9 7 5 3 1

For more information or to place bulk orders, contact the publisher at Jennifer@BrightCommunications.net.

To my sweet daughter, Maggie Lyn: I hope this book inspires you to know that you can follow and achieve your dreams.

CONTENTS

INTRODUCTION

FINDING FREEDOM FROM CLUTTER—FINALLY!

Imagine walking into a cluttered, disorganized, dusty room. What feelings do you have?

Now picture walking in the front door of a sparkling clean, orderly, minimalist space. There is a major difference in the feelings and thoughts that these two extremes produce. Too much physical clutter can take over, leaving us feeling distracted and stressed. When we have extra clutter in our homes, offices, and home offices, we can experience a cluttered mind. Increases in stress negatively impact our productivity and wellness. Clutter gets in between you and the life you want to live.

Decluttering is a task that needs to be done regularly, like laundry or bathing. You don't organize one day, and then you're set for life. (If only!) You'll likely find that once you are finished organizing one area, it is time to start organizing somewhere else. Consider your new, decluttered life a work in progress.

Before we delve into decluttering specific rooms in your home and organizing particular items, I'll share one of my favorite overall organizing strategies: One In, One Out. If you bring something into your home, get rid of something else to make room. For example, when you go clothes shopping for clothes and bring home a few new things, fill those empty shopping bags with old clothes and take them to a donation center.

Another overall mindset shift is: When you are at a store, remember all of the hard work you are putting into decluttering your space. Don't undo that work by buying more things!

As you read this book, remember that not every tip works for every family. It's always important to take the best and leave the rest. Try to choose at least one tip from each section in this book that you can put into action immediately and wholeheartedly.

For me, committing to a minimalist mindset greatly helped me declutter. It helped me to let go of items that no longer serve me, and it encourages me to be free of unnecessary clutter.

Often, we hold onto items out of fear—the fear of loss, the fear that we might need an item sometime in the future—even if we haven't used it in years. In order to be free from clutter, we have to explore the fears that are preventing us from letting go of the items that no longer serve us.

But it's worth all of the work! Finding freedom from clutter helps us lead more rewarding, productive lives. If you make decluttering a habit, the process will become easier and easier.

When we liberate ourselves from the clutter in our personal and work lives, we open up space for creativity, productivity, and joy! Join me on the wonderful journey of finding freedom from clutter!

ORGANIZING YOUR GOALS

Let's take some time to talk about goal setting. Setting goals can be such a rewarding experience. Just writing goals down gives me an energy boost and a bunch of motivation. I remember when I was first starting out in business and a coach encouraged me to write down goals that I had. I even typed up a list of six-month, one-year, three-year, and five-year goals and posted them onto my wall so that I would see them every day. And guess what? Many of these written goals came to fruition. Having clarity about what I really wanted allowed me to have a supercharged 2017, when I got married, started my business, bought a house with my husband, and even adopted a second dog. (That goal was more my husband's, but I do love our dog Annie..

However, it is very easy to achieve one goal and not set a new one. Recently I started another program with the same coach, and I realized that this year I didn't set any goals at all. I began to realize that this could be the cause of the recent lack of excitement and enthusiasm that I have been experiencing. After setting a few goals and quickly jotting them down on Post-it Notes, I felt immediately energized and excited about doing the work to achieve them. There is something powerful about goal-setting, and it can be a huge catalyst for change in your life. If you want to do big things in life, start by setting goals and writing them down. And take a few of my favorite tips on Goal Setting to Super Charge!

Get into the habit of achieving your goals. When you achieve a goal, it gives you a boost and satisfaction that makes you want to go after other goals in your life. This can create a snowball effect. For example, if you want to live a healthier lifestyle, meeting a goal to eat more fruits and vegetables might inspire you to next add more physical activity into your routine. Creating good habits to become more organized works the same away. Set small goals to start. Rather than deciding to reorganize your entire house, start with just one room or even just one drawer. If you want to better organize your finances, look at how and what you spend and make a few small, but meaningful, changes. For example, switch to a few generic brands at the grocery store or get takeout one less time per month.

Write your goals down. Writing down your goals and reviewing them every day gets you into the habit of visualizing your goals and taking the steps necessary to see them to the finish line. Keep your written goals somewhere you will be able to see them frequently. A planner, a print-out that hangs inside your bathroom cabinet, or a whiteboard in your home office are just a few places where you will see your goals constantly, keeping you on task.

Furthermore, breaking down goals into short-term and long-term, and writing down the steps necessary to achieve them has helped me, so I know firsthand that it can help you as well. Whether you want to sell a certain number of products or want to organize your house from top to bottom, creating a list of tangible to-do items and reviewing it often can help make those changes happen.

I did this when I was downsizing my parent's 13-acre farm. I created a list of specific things that needed to happen, and then I listed the steps in order to make each one a reality. This process gave me clarity, and it also allowed me to delegate certain tasks to my helpers, which was essential to finishing by our deadline, which was closing day on the sale of the property.

Share your goals with others. Much of my childhood was focused on dance, but after I graduated high school, I stopped dancing for almost 10 years. It was not until I started working with another coach, time and stress management expert Ryan Dunphy, that I realized I wanted to start dancing again. I told him my goal, and he helped me break it down into smaller steps. Then by chance, I ran into a local dance teacher while we were walking our dogs, and she said that she offered an adult tap class—and the class was that night! I was really nervous, but I posted on my Facebook page, "Wish me luck, I'm going to tap class!" The positive support I got from friends and family was overwhelming and motivated me even more to recapture my love of dancing. Believe me, once you post a goal for all of your Facebook friends to see, it is very hard to back out.

Once you set a goal, be vulnerable and share it in every way possible. Post it on all your social media. Text or, better yet, call people whose opinions matter to you and tell them about it. Ask for their help in holding you accountable. I promise you, it will be well worth it.

Make it fun. Friendly competition makes things fun. For example, kids who don't like to do chores are more likely to do them when it becomes a competition. Whoever can pick up the most toys gets a cookie!

You can make your goal-achieving process fun by turning it into a game. Apps like Habitica make goal attainment feel like playing a video game. You can create a point system that equates to the necessary actions you will need to take in order to reach your goal. Points are fun, but rewards are better; if you score 'X' number of points, that triggers a fun reward for you. While the reward can vary from person to person, ideally you will want to make the reward relevant to your overarching goals. That connection will make the reward that much more impactful

Be kind to yourself. There's a reason why New Year's resolutions fail to stick. It takes patience and persistence and also kindness toward yourself. Does this sound familiar? You set a goal for yourself to eat healthier and lose weight. After a couple weeks of eating better meals, you cave to your sweet tooth and have a bowl of waffle cone ice cream for dessert. Immediately after eating it, you feel bad that you broke your healthy streak. Suddenly, the seeds of doubt begin to creep in about your ability to stay true to your goal. With just one dessert and a lack of kindness toward yourself for breaking your healthy eating habit just once, you let your negative thoughts prevail, your goal falls by the wayside, and the healthy improvements you made begin to go backward.

Every step of the goal attainment process involves stress. It's how you manage that stress that will help you adjust when things don't go your way, either by your own doing or someone else's actions. Rather than sulking when things don't go well, reframe your mindset to accept the fact that setbacks happen and that you'll be stronger for having gone through them.

A great book called *Say Goodbye to Survival Mode* by Crystal Paine emphasizes the key reason behind setting goals—namely, to make you a better person, not to destroy your self-worth.

Whether it be during the New Year holiday or any other time throughout the year, I encourage you to take the time to look at yourself honestly and with kindness, and to identify ways that you would like to be better this year and beyond. And don't worry if it takes longer than you'd expect. Life is a marathon, not a sprint. If it helps (and I think it will!), you can download my Project Planning Board PDF at https://hereforyoupa.com/blog to help you identify your goals and begin the process of making them a reality.

ORGANIZING AROUND THE HOUSE

Our houses are our hub of family life. Above my door we have a sign that says "Family, where life begins and the love never ends." Our homes are a reflection of what is inside ourselves. When we have harmony in the home, everything just feels better. And the opposite is also true. A home should be a sanctuary from the outside world, not another obstacle to overcome. It is true that children and pets can make decluttering more of a challenge; it is still possible to have balance. There is a difference between being a little messy and having a cluttered home. Sometimes too many decorations, unnecessary kitchen items, an overabundance of clothing and toys can literally take over a home. If you are experiencing stress and overwhelm in your home, it may be time to take a hard look at your possessions and decide whether they are serving you, or you are serving them.

ORGANIZING THE KITCHEN

Whether you are a busy parent, working many hours per week, or simply tired at the end of a long day, becoming organized in the kitchen can be a saving grace. Happiness in the kitchen starts with organization! Read on for my top tips and tricks to guide you into organizing recipes, creating a meal planning binder, and storing kitchen essentials.

Organize by zone. When you are organizing your kitchen, consider the different purposes that you use the kitchen for. Begin with the end in mind. Do you like to cook a lot, or are you only cooking occasionally? Do you drink tea or coffee or mainly water from the fridge? Do you need certain appliances every day or are there appliances you use only for special occasions? Write down your answers and organize your kitchen in a way that works well for you.

For example, I drink a lot of tea and coffee, so in my kitchen I have a dedicated coffee and tea cabinet where I keep all my coffee accessories and coffee cups. I could have put coffee cups with other cups, but because I use them so often and have so many of them, it makes more sense to keep them organized with the coffee items.

Another example is baking items. I had one client who loved to bake on the weekends with her young daughters. She had baking items in many different places throughout the kitchen. So I suggested dedicating one specific drawer for the many sets of measuring cups and spoons. Also, I set up a pantry cabinet that had all of the dry ingredients they needed to get baking. That way when it was time to bake, everything was in one place. This encourages more baking!

Make it stack. A kitchen organizing tip that is often overlooked is stacking items. I love my French glass nesting bowls because eight different sized bowls only take up the space of the largest bowl. The same goes for food storage. If you invest in a set of lidded, glass storage containers that are different sizes but all the same shape, such as Pyrex or Anchor Hocking, you will be able to stack to your heart's content without taking up a large footprint in your kitchen.

I learned about this from visiting my grandmother's house in Florida. My grandmother and my aunt have only round glass storage bowls, and it helps keep food storage clutter to a minimum. We all know how frustrating it is to have 30 different storage containers with different sized and shaped lids. Declare Tupperware bankruptcy: Get rid all of the mismatched pieces, and get a new set. You will thank me.

Be ruthless about kitchen clutter. Kitchens love to collect stuff. We enjoy buying new kitchen items, but too often these items are seldom used. When we see that microplane on a TV show, we want one, too. And so it begins. Soon you have kitchen accessories in every nook and cranny, and you think you need more storage. In my experience, more storage can help, but in reality you have to stop buying new stuff. Celebrity chef Alton Brown is famous for his one-man crusade against the dreaded "uni-taskers" of the kitchen. The more gadgets and doodads that you have in the kitchen, the less organized you are.

When helping my clients organize their homes, I have found many high-quality kitchen items in their original boxes, forgotten in the basement. What is not remembered, is not missed! Do family and friends give you kitchen gadgets, knowing you like to cook? Have a discussion about how you want to keep the kitchen organized and you need their help. If you can't do this, make a box for everything they give you and take it right to the local donation center. (For information on donating unneeded things, see "Donating Your Stuff" on page 32.)

Organize your pantry. A particularly challenging area of the kitchen to keep organized is the pantry. A bonus to having an organized pantry that is not stuffed to the brim is that it is easier to clean. Here are my top tips.

• Use up and clean out food on a regular basis. Grocery shopping day is a great time to use up anything left over from the last week.

• Throw away food that you know isn't going to get used by the expiration date. You always want to have a variety of pantry items on hand, and you want to know that nothing is expired. If you've ever tried to use an expired baking mix, only to find out that it does not rise, you know how frustrating it can be!

• Place boxes, such as crackers and pasta, on their sides or stack them to get some more space.

• Keep a clear bin in your pantry cabinet to hold little snack items. I buy a large bag of nuts or dried fruit and put smaller portions into my snack bin in containers or plastic snack bags. This makes packing lunches much easier on busy mornings!

• Stack cans two high if possible.

• Store heavy cans on the bottom shelf.

• Place new items behind older ones so you can make sure you are using the oldest first.

• A good rule of thumb for the pantry and other areas is "When it's full, empty it, and when it's empty, fill it!"

Make a recipe binder. A recipe binder is a compilation of greatest hits of all of the best recipes from your collection of cookbooks or printed recipes from the internet. Having everything you love to cook in one place makes meal planning easy because you can scan the binder for meals you've made before. You can find your favorite recipes all in one place, and you don't need to keep all of the cookbooks in the kitchen, which makes more room for cooking! You can make notes on your recipes about any alterations you made, how your family liked the recipe and what you might do differently next time.

This is a great system for keeping your recipes organized and accessible, and you can personalize your binder by making a custom cover or using colorful dividers!

To make a recipe binder, you'll need:
• Three-ring binder
• Tab dividers
• Clear page protectors
• Your favorite cookbooks
• Your favorite printed recipes
• Photocopier (If you don't have one, go to the local library or office supply store.)

Step 1: Photocopy your favorite recipes or print them from the internet.

Step 2: Organize the recipes into piles in categories that make sense to you, such as by protein (beef, chicken, pork) and beverages, side dishes, salads, and desserts.

Step 3: If desired, further sort the recipes in each category into alphabetical order.

Step 4: Insert two recipes, back to back, into each pocket protector.

Step 5: Label the tab dividers with your categories.

Step 6: Place the tab dividers and recipes into your binder.

Step 7: Get cooking!

Getting organized in the kitchen can help streamline meal planning and cooking meals at home. When your food and tools are accessible and visible, it is easier to find what you need without pulling everything out of the cabinets and making an even bigger mess! Having some organization will allow you to keep things cleaner and make cooking quicker and easier.

Imagine a restaurant with a disorganized, cluttered kitchen. Would you want to eat there? Take inspiration from open-air kitchens when organizing your own. It may take some hard work and time to get your kitchen to where you want it to be. Don't be afraid to reach out to a local Professional Organizer if you need a hand! The time and energy will pay dividends and result in more delicious family meals that create memories around the table.

ORGANIZING YOUR FRIDGE AND FREEZER

If there is one area of the home that gets the most attention, it's the fridge and freezer. Certainly in my home, whenever someone is hungry or bored, they naturally gravitate towards the fridge, looking to see if there is anything interesting to snack on.

Where some families run into trouble is not keeping up with the fridge, either letting things overstay their welcome or packing things in too tightly. I prefer to have the fridge only 50 to 75 percent full, with everything easily visible. We eat with our eyes after all, so being able to see everything at a glance is key to proper fridge organization. When the fridge looks clean and inviting, we are more likely to eat the groceries we have purchased, reducing food and money wasted. With grocery prices on the rise, we can all appreciate the need to have organization and systems within our fridges and freezers! Read some of my favorite tips to keep these high-traffic areas efficient, organized, and clean.

Follow the first in, first out rule. Food waste is a huge problem in the United States. According to the USDA, the average American family of four throws out approximately $1,500 in food per year. When planning your meals in preparation for grocery shopping, think first about what you have in the fridge. Sometimes fridges get packed, and the older groceries get pushed to the back, but it is ideal to rotate what is in your fridge. Place the newest items in the back, and bring the older things to the front. You might notice the stockers doing this at the grocery store. When you practice FIFO (first in first out), you will use things up instead of letting them go to waste.

Wait to shop until you're almost out. I love to do my grocery shopping on the same day each week, but if there are still a lot of groceries to use, it might be a good idea to wait a few days. This allows you to get through what you have instead of packing more items into the fridge and burying the older items.

Use leftovers. Can you make a meal with the rest of last week's veggies and a meat item from the freezer? I like to make meals I call "universal receivers," which can be made using almost any leftover proteins and vegetables you have in the fridge. Some examples of universal receivers are fried rice, omelets, noodle bowls, salads, pizza and tacos. An added bonus of making these meals is you empty the fridge shelves, so you can clean the shelves when they are almost empty, while reducing your food waste.

Limit your condiments. Sometimes I am amazed with the sheer number of condiments I see in fridges. When I was younger, my family had a fridge full of way too many different jars and random sauces for specific dishes. They never got used up, and they sat around— sometimes for years. Yuck! When an opportunity came to actually use that mango chutney, I was never sure how old it was, and I ended up throwing it away.

Pro tip: Make condiments yourself. For example, tartar sauce is just mayo with a bit of relish, and cocktail sauce is just ketchup with a bit of horseradish. Unless you eat seafood all of the time, it might be easier to make a small batch of homemade tartar sauce or cocktail sauce while you're cooking instead of keeping so many extra jars in the fridge. The same goes for salad dressings. In my house, I prefer to have no more than two or three varieties of salad dressing in my fridge at a time. If I want something different, I wait until one runs out and then change it up. Some salad dressings are easily made from scratch as well, with a few simple ingredients. Got an almost empty bottle of Dijon mustard? Add some oil and vinegar to make a Dijon Vinaigrette. It is very easy to find recipes for almost any dressing or condiment online, and you'll likely find that you already have many of the ingredients on hand.

Make lunch-overs. Growing up, another thing that bothered me about our fridge is that we didn't use many of our leftovers. With good intentions, we would put our leftovers in separate Tupperware containers for another day, but they would usually be forgotten until they started to smell bad and got tossed away. Today, I avoid this by making "lunch-overs," which are pre-portioned leftovers in silicone lunch containers that can be quickly microwaved at home or at work. I like silicone containers for meal prep because many of them are collapsable, meaning they take up less space in cabinets, and they come in fun colors which is an added bonus. My containers are divided in the middle so that if I have a starch on one side it stays separate from the protein on the other. When we have leftovers, I grab these containers, cut up any meat, and portion out several lunches. Making them interesting can be as simple as using barbeque sauce on one chicken rice bowl and mustard on another one. You can use rice left over from Chinese takeout with chicken left over from a crockpot meal and add a vegetable for a complete meal. In the morning when we are running around, we can easily toss these into a lunch bag and go. This way things get used up and wasted much less often.

When in doubt, throw it out. Sometimes leftovers just don't look great. They are starting to change colors or have dried out. At this point, don't delay throwing it away. Most food will only stay good once cooked for about five to seven days. You may feel a bit guilty since you are wasting food, but if you leave it in there, it will take up valuable real estate and probably not get eaten anyway. It is better to get rid of it rather than leave it for another family member to stumble upon. They will still have to throw it away. Also, you might risk food-borne illness if someone does eat it by mistake. It is nearly impossible to eat 100 percent of what we bring home, so sometimes this is a necessary step.

Clean it out. Sometimes a fridge gets so cluttered, it needs a complete overhaul. Often clients ask me to clean out their fridges for them. I am happy to oblige. I love the look of a clean fridge. If your fridge has not been cleaned in some time, it may take on the smells of old food, which may make things go bad more quickly. Some fridges even come equipped with an air filter, which needs to be changed out at certain intervals. One way to keep the smells from accumulating is to use baking soda, either a small bowl or the Fridge Pack. When tasked with cleaning out the fridge, I always check the dates on food items and almost always find a few things that have expired. Many times when removing the produce drawers I will find sticky spills that have been forgotten about. It is important to regularly maintain and clean these areas. A clean fridge is a healthy fridge!

An important reason to declutter your fridge and freezer is that most food has a certain window of use. Even frozen food deteriorates and loses quality if it sits too long. While many people like to keep food stored for a rainy day, it is important to be realistic about the limitations of food storage. Having a system for organizing your fridge and freezer is key to getting the most value out of the food in your home. If you need some extra help organizing your fridge or freezer, reach out to Here For You Concierge or another home management pro in your local area. Having a second person provide honest, open feedback can help with the decision-making process and make the process quicker and easier. Now it's time to go get yourself a snack from the fridge!

ORGANIZING YOUR CLOTHES CLOSETS

One of the simplest places to start organizing is in your clothes closets because we are very in touch with our clothing. Typically, you go into the closet every day to find what you will wear, so it is easy to have a sense of what is being used and what is just taking up space.

On the other hand, what makes closets difficult to organize is the attachment that we can have to items that we no longer fit, expensive items we've never worn, or things that we like but don't actually have an occasion to wear. The more clothing a person has, the harder it often is for them to let go of some things.

Here's an example. I love to watch old episodes of *Wife Swap*. Many times on the show, women have entire rooms full of clothing, and they are often very attached to their things. In one episode, a New Jersey self-proclaimed high-maintenance mom swapped lives with a mom who lives in a rustic cabin in the woods with no electricity. On the show, the moms each set rules for the other household. One of the rustic mom's rules was for each of the high-maintenance mom's family members to donate seven items of clothing. The high-maintenance mom was very upset at this rule because she had spent so much money on her daughter's clothes. She flipped out at the episode's family meeting, and she almost left the show.

Yes, it can be tough getting rid of clothing because what we wear is so closely tied to our sense of identity. So, here are a few tips to get you started clearing out your closet.

Grab some bags. Before you start, have a few kitchen garbage bags handy. Ideally grab bags in two different colors: one color for items to sell and the other color for items to donate.

In my experience, most people will need more than one bag for donations. Some of my clients fill seven to 10 bags with clothing to donate! One of my clients loves to fill 55 gallon drums of her old clothing and send them overseas to Jamaica, where they are distributed to people in need. It's a good idea to have another container handy for items that need repairs, such as sewing a fallen hem or replacing a lost button. Try to get those things to a tailor asap. (For information on donating unneeded things, see "Donating Your Stuff" on page 32.)

Take everything out. The next step of cleaning out a closet is to empty the closet completely. Move everything out of your closet onto your bed or another large surface. It's not ideal, but if need be, this can be done in stages. While your closet is empty, vacuum, wipe shelves, and dust corners/baseboards before putting everything back.

Gather clothing stored elsewhere. In addition to your closet, do you store clothing in other places, such as your basement? Bring that clothing to your bed, too. It helps if you know how much stuff you need to store in order to get everything to fit. If your clothes are over-flowing into the guest room closet or even the basement (eek!), it could be a good goal to get rid of enough so that your main closet will fit all of your clothing. Assess how much you need to pare down in order to accomplish this. Sometimes it helps my clients to think of things in percentages, so I'll suggest that they get rid of a third of what they have in order to fit it into the space we are working with.

Go through everything item by item. As you go through your items, remember your goal to get organized. Keep your eye on the prize! This will help you gauge how you are doing. One at a time, pick up a piece of clothing and really look at it. Handling each item serves two purposes:

• It allows you to make a decision on whether or not you will wear it again.

• It allows you to remember everything you have in your closet.

Most people wear only a small fraction of what is in their closet on a daily basis. If it's been a few years since you were able to get to the back of your closet, you probably don't have a clue what is actually there. What's not remembered is not missed, so seeing everything again will help you use things that you didn't know you had—or get rid of things you never missed! As you assess each item, either place it back on your bed, into the bag of items to sell, into the bag of items to donate, or into the container of items needing repairs.

Move the bags. Once you've assessed each item of clothing, tie the bag(s) of items to sell and items to donate and get them out of the room either by selling or donating. You could place the bag(s) of items to donate right in your car. If you plan to sell items, do it quickly so they don't become extra clutter. (For more information on donating and selling unneeded things, see "Donating Your Stuff" on page 32 and "Selling Your Stuff" on page 28.)

Group items into categories. Now that your closet has "thrown up" all over your bed, organize the items into categories. For example, pile all of your short-sleeved T-shirts in the top left corner of your bed, long-sleeved T-shirts at the top middle, sweaters in the top right corner, shorts in the bottom left, pants in the bottom, and jeans in the bottom right corner. If items are spilling out onto the floor, don't worry, you'll be picking them up soon.

Put things back by category. Think about how you'd like to store those categories in your closet. If you're looking for a red cardigan, for example, would you be more likely to look for it in a section of cardigans or in a section of red clothing? Some clients like to keep things simple, and others like to have a bunch of different categories. Think of how you will access your clothing. My tip to clients is to not over-categorize things. This can be unnecessary and make the process of putting things back from the laundry more difficult, which is the last thing you want! Stick to a few big categories and make your life easier down the line.

Decide to hang or fold. Some people love to hang all of their clothing, including pants. It really depends on how your closet is laid out and how much room you have. Most people want to have a mixture with some things hanging and others folded. Obviously you are not going to hang underwear and socks! Personally, I like to hang anything that wrinkles easily, and I fold less-likely-to-wrinkle T-shirts and pants.

Store seasonal clothing. Seasonal clothing can be a challenge, especially if you live in the Northeast or somewhere similar where temperatures vary widely between seasons. If you locate seasonal clothing somewhere other than your closet, you might forget about it and then buy more of the same things, which will then take up more space in your home.

A few months ago when I was cleaning out the closet in my office, I found a bunch of my husband's winter thermals that I had forgotten about. To avoid this scenario, I recommend keeping seasonal clothes close and accessible. If you have some room in the back of your regular closet, that is a great place. Another option is to place seasonal clothing in vacuum storage bags and store them on a shelf in your closet or under your bed—somewhere that they won't be forgotten.

Clothing closet organizing is very popular. I have worked with clients with closets of all shapes and sizes. The important thing to remember is that if you have too much clothing, it makes things infinitely harder to organize. (This applies to other things as well.) Having too much clothing also makes laundry more difficult. You can put it off longer, making the piles larger and turning it into an unmanageable task. Also, you might find that it is easier to get dressed and look good each day when you are not overwhelmed by too many options.

Personally, I have cut down my clothing a lot over the years. I have had to make intentional changes to my behavior like reducing the amount of incoming email ads for my favorite clothing stores, not going to the mall unless I really need something, and spending less time flipping through fashion magazines. Doing these things allowed me to place less emphasis on clothing and fashion in my life. While I still have a good amount of clothing options from which to choose, I don't have clothing overflowing from my closest. Still, a few times a year I need to take a good look at my closet and get rid of things I am no longer wearing. If finding freedom from clutter is important to you, starting with the clothes in your closet is a good place.

ORGANIZING YOUR BASEMENT OR GARAGE

My largest organizing projects are typically for clients asking for help organizing their basements and garages. These areas are a catch-all for items like sports equipment, camping gear, and kid's items, as well as tools and household maintenance supplies.

When these items get used, they have a valid reason to remain. But many times, things are kept that haven't been used in years—if not decades.

It can be very difficult to get rid of items that were very expensive at the time of purchase, or items that bring back fond memories of family fun and togetherness. But basements and garages fill up quickly, and when that happens they become difficult and over-whelming to deal with. Another challenge of storing items in a basement or garage is the environment. Temperatures can fluctuate, and sometimes they become damp, which can lead to mold growth. It is very easy for items to be ruined under these conditions.

Many of these tips also apply to offsite storage units, which are really just auxiliary basements and garages.

Move items you should never keep in the basement or garage. The first step in organizing your basement or garage is removing the following items that should not be there in the first place.

Photos. Your precious photos should never be stored in the basement or garage—or the attic for that matter, especially if they have not been digitized or properly backed up. The experts at the Association of Professional Photo Managers recommend that they be stored somewhere in the main level of the house. Through the Photo Managers Facebook Group, I read a story about a woman who lost all her wedding photos due to the damage caused by a hurricane. Her photos were stored in her basement, which flooded. As she lamented about the loss on social media, her cousin messaged her to say she had a copy of the woman's wedding video. In this case she was able to recover some of her memories, but not everyone is this lucky!

Pro tip: I recommend the 3-2-1 rule for backing up your photos:

- *Keep 3 different copies*
- *In 2 different formats*
- *With 1 copy offsite*

For example, you could have your photos stored on two different USBs and on Cloud Storage. Or you could have an external hard drive, Cloud Storage, and the original photos. If the thought of accomplishing this makes your head spin, it may be time to contact a local photo manager to walk you through this process. These pros can scan your original images using a high-resolution scanner and store and back them up on a Cloud-based service.

Clothes. Like photos, clothes do not store well in the basement. Unless they are inside air-tight totes or vacuum storage bags, clothes in the basement in trash bags or other non-airtight containers will take on the basement's smell. You are not likely to be able to wear those clothes again. If you have so much clothing that it will not all fit into your bedroom closet, it might be time for a major clothing declutter! Pare down seasonal clothes to what you really need. Find somewhere closer to your bedroom closet to keep these things. As I mentioned before, if you don't, you might forget you have them when the season comes to wear them and end up buying them again.

Memorabilia. Old newspapers or magazines that capture important moments in time need to be digitized and backed up. If the originals are important, they should be put in archival containers and kept anywhere but the basement or garage—or attic. As for any personal memorabilia that you have in the basement—like that Thanksgiving turkey that your daughter, who now has kids of her own, made for you in second grade using her handprint—I recommend camera scanning them. Take photos of the special pieces you want to remember and ditch the rest. You can even organize the photos into a unique photo album.

Relocate some items to your basement or garage. Now that you've moved photos, clothing, and memorabilia out of your basement or garage, you hopefully have cleared some space for some items that are more appropriately stored in your basement or garage.

Old kids' toys. If you decided to hang onto your kids' toys for your future grandchildren, you could keep them in the basement. Make sure they are stored in plastic totes or vacuum storage bags.

But let's get real, if you were planning on keeping your kids' toys with the intent of selling them one day on eBay, unless your kids' toys are still in their original packaging, they aren't worth much. Don't plan on getting top dollar for them. Unless you have experience selling on eBay and will follow through on your good intentions, you're better off getting rid of them. Take them to a reputable eBay consignor, hold a yard sale, or simply donate them. (For more information on selling unneeded items, see "Selling Your Stuff" on page 28.)

Collectibles. From Hummel figurines, to Department 56 houses, (Christmas house, Snowbabies, etc.) to Longaberger baskets, my clients have invested in all kinds of unique collectibles, often with the hope that those items would have a return on investment. However, if these items are not stored properly in the basement, they will get ruined and have the value of a used paper plate. Even if kept in good condition, many of these "collectors items" were mass produced and therefore not particularly rare or valuable.

According to the antiques buyers I work with, items that most people think are valuable are not, and some items that people think are junk can be very valuable. One example of this is ephemera, which are paper antiques. Our estate buyer shared a story of when he dug through the bin at a farm and found letters, which he offered to buy. Once he was able to research their origin it turned out they were from the Civil War and worth a pretty penny.

Holiday decorations. Another basement staple, the holiday decorations you use regularly should be stored properly, and you should get rid of the rest. Nothing accumulates quite like holiday décor, and it will take some commitment to weed out the decorations that you haven't used in years. Remember FIFO, First In First Out. One exception that's in style right now is vintage holiday decor. Do you have a ceramic Christmas tree somewhere in your basement? Most of us do. If your holiday decorations look worn or out of style, it's time to say goodbye. Be realistic about what you are actually going to use. Think of it this way: If an item stays in storage for 11 months out of the year, it should definitely be getting used for the one month a year that it is relevant!

One holiday item you can get rid of right away is extra, new holiday cards. These cards fall into the category of "donate ASAP." If you're like me, you keep a list of people to whom you send cards, but chances are you have boxes of leftover cards in your basement that you used in years past. Was it last year or the year before? Save the guess-work and donate them. You will spare yourself the trouble of having to unstick the glue that has become sealed due to the humidity in the basement. (For more information on organizing holiday décor, see "Organizing for the Holidays" on page 49.)

Electronics: You can store both new and old devices in the basement or garage if they are stored properly. But before you store your elec-tronics, always remove the batteries. Batteries lose their power over time, and they can become corroded, which could damage your device. You can recycle old batteries at community electronics collec-tion events in your area or at places like Batteries+.

Party supplies. When deciding whether to keep your leftover party supplies, think about when you will use them again. If something is super specific like 50th birthday napkins or jungle theme paper plates, it is probably best to use these up in your kitchen or to donate them. But if you have a lot of children and your party supplies can be reused for the next child's party, it is okay to store them. Keep everything together in a plastic tote and try to use them up at the next event. After a few years, paper party supplies can become warped and not so presentable for your guests.

Read before storing! Paint, lawn chemicals, and other hazardous materials are often kept in the basement because the temperature is generally cooler than somewhere like the garage or shed, and people rightfully worry about anything potentially flammable being exposed to warmer climates. Read the instructions on every hazardous material you have in your house and decide where best to keep it safely and securely—especially away from children.

When disposing of hazardous material, follow the instructions to the letter as well. Often it involves contacting your city or local municipality, who will tell you how to dispose of the material properly. Some areas offer special drop-off events for people with hazardous materials. For instance, Habitat for Humanity's ReStore periodically holds latex paint collection events. They can actually make new paints out of the old ones collected. Taking the extra time and energy to dispose of these things properly will help keep them out of waterways and away from wildlife.

Other Best Practices for Basement Storage

• Plastic totes and vacuum storage bags are great ways to keep your basement items odor-free, safe, and intact.

• For added moisture protection in your plastic totes, add one or two silica gel packs that you get when you buy, for example, a pair of shoes. These will absorb any extra moisture. They also work great for drying out your smartphone if it gets wet! You can also buy these in bulk on Amazon.

• Another basement best practice is using the right type of shelving. I recommend Metro shelving (like the kind you see in the food service industry or on shows like *CutThroat Kitchen*). These shelving units are sturdy, long-lasting, and resilient to basement conditions. The ability to adjust shelves to fit your storage containers is an added bonus with Metro shelving.

• When shopping for shelving for your basement, consider the condition of your basement (finished versus unfinished) as well as the weight of the items that you will be storing on the shelves. While plastic shelving units are the least expensive, heavy items can cause bowing and warping. Look for shelves in which the bottom shelf sits a few inches off the ground, especially if you get water in your basement. The slight elevation can be enough to lessen the possibility of your items getting wet.

Basements and garages don't have to be a dumping ground for long-forgotten things. If you stay realistic about the things you will use in the future, versus things you are holding onto just because, you can make better decisions about what to keep and what to get rid of. Keep in mind that some items do not store well in basement conditions and there are best practices for storage and shelving.

If you are totally overwhelmed by the prospect of cleaning out these areas, don't be afraid to call in backup. Whether it be friends and family or a professional organizer, big projects warrant a team effort. The longer you procrastinate, the harder it may become. Take the first step to get organized in the basement and find freedom from basement clutter!

SELLING, DONATING, AND DISCARDING YOUR CLUTTER

I wish I had a magic wand that could make your cabinets, closets, basements, and houses bigger! But alas, I do not. So, an important part of decluttering is actually getting rid of stuff that you don't need.

There are three ways to do this: Sell it, donate it, or discard it. Let's talk about each in turn.

SELLING YOUR STUFF

There are several options to sell items you no longer need or want, including yard sales, websites like Facebook Marketplace and eBay, and consignment stores.

Yard Sales

Yard sales have a proven track record for several reasons. They are effective at helping to declutter your home or office, the items being sold are going where someone will appreciate them, and you can make a little money, too! Here's how.

Plan the right date. Think about when you see the most yard sales in your area. Are spring and summer more popular than fall? Are most sales on Saturdays or Sundays? Do you want to hold a one-, two-, or even three-day sale? How much time realistically do you need to gather items to sell and clean them if necessary? Give yourself plenty of time so you can make the most of your time preparing for and holding the yard sale.

If you are lucky enough to live in a town that hosts a community yard sale day, make sure to take advantage of it. These are great opportunities because many folks come out for events like this, and you may get more traffic

If your yard or garage aren't well suited for a yard sale, for instance if parking isn't allowed on your street or if you don't want to have people come to your home, consider joining another sale. Local churches might also have a yard sale where you can bring your own stuff and rent a table or two.

Follow the rules. Be sure to contact your township to ensure you are complying with the local yard sale regulations. You might have to pay a small fee to hold the sale. Ask about rules for advertising your sale, too.

Get the word out. The important thing to remember is that you need to get the word out! To attract buyers to your sale, I suggest advertising in the local paper, on Facebook Marketplace, and on Craigslist. You can also place signs on telephone poles, as long as it is ok with local regulations and you remove them when the sale is finished! Always check your local municipality to make sure they allow this.

Get up early. Be prepared for yard sale hobbyists who will show up early, with cash, ready to buy if they see something they want.

Price things to sell. Go for volume over getting top dollar for things. Your goal should be to get rid of things, not to hold out for a higher price. Freedom from clutter is your reward at the end; the money you make is just icing on the cake. Don't forget to make sure your items look clean by doing a basic bare minimum cleaning. This will greatly help in selling your items. Whatever is not sold at the end should be placed on curb alert or taken to the closest donation center. You can make this easier on yourself by scheduling a donation pickup far in advance for the day after the yard sale.

Websites

Other great resources for selling things are local groups such as Facebook Marketplace, NextDoor, LetGo, 5 Miles, and Craigslist.

Facebook Marketplace can be a great resource with nicer things such as brand name furniture and clothing. Online auctions like eBay are great if you are willing to pack and ship your items to the buyer. They have a mobile app that makes it very quick and easy to list your items for sale, and you can use their "Sell One Like This" feature to quickly generate the content for your ad.

Here are some tips to keep in mind when selling online.

Be persistent. It takes more time and effort than selling everything at a yard sale because you have to create individual listings, take photos, write descriptions, answer questions from buyers, and meet up with the buyers. But you will generally get higher prices for your items.

Always keep safety in mind. Choose meetup locations in public places and make sure someone else is aware if you are having a stranger come to your home. If you get a bad feeling, don't give out your address. Most sites offer the ability to check the other person's profile, but you never know if that is really who will be coming.

Stores

Many different types of consignment stores will consign or buy your items to sell. Some examples include the following.

• Music stores that buy vinyl, instruments, and CDs

• Clothing consignors or stores like Plato's Closet that buy for cash.

• Children's consignment stores that accept clothes, toys and other kids items

• Stores that buy used sports equipment

• Wedding dress and special occasion dress consignment

• Book stores that pay cash for used books, video games, and DVDs

• Music stores that buy instruments and used equipment

• Antiques stores that buy or consign items

If items that you are getting rid of are nice enough, and recent enough, you may be able to sell them on consignment. Some stores even offer you cash or store credit for your old things. While this can be very time-consuming, it can be rewarding. Here are my top tips.

Call first. Before you go to a store to consign, make sure that your items meet their parameters. It is no fun lugging big bags of stuff from the car into the store, only to have to lug them all back out again. Many of these stores post their guidelines on their websites.

Go online. Some companies now offer online consignment, so you will just ship your items to them in mailing bags that they supply. But the same thing applies here, make sure what you are sending meets recent guidelines. Even if you paid a lot for clothes that are 10-15 years old, they probably won't sell if you send them to one of these companies.

If your items are old enough, or vintage, you may be able to sell them to a vintage store. Again, these places look for specific styles and time periods, so call ahead before you make the trek.

Hire help. If online selling feels overwhelming, you could work with an eBay consigner who sells general merchandise. This takes a lot of the headaches and time out of selling these things.

Try an auction. If your items are vintage or antiques, your best bet might be to sell it at an auction via an auctioneer. Here in the Lehigh Valley, we are lucky to have many local auction houses and auctioneers. Some of them specialize in high-end items, and others are generalists that will take all types of items. You might need to do some research and call around to find the best auction house for your needs —or have a concierge do this research for you.

A possible drawback with selling items at auction is that you cannot control the final selling price. However, many auctioneers let you set a reserve price or starting bid if you want to get at least a certain amount for your stuff. Selling this way can be easier and less time consuming than a yard sale or selling on a local group, but make sure you know what to expect. Once an item is sold at auction, there is no getting it back.

If you have an entire house full of items to sell, consider working with an estate buyer. These pros will come to your location and make offers on antiques in your home. They often look for mid-century modern furniture, jewelry, and other items that are in demand in the antiques market. But if you are trying to downsize, this could be a quick, easy way to get some cash for your things. Find these pros in your local area on Craigslist under the "wanted" section.

DONATING YOUR STUFF

For items in good condition that you don't need or want, donation is the quickest, easiest way to get rid of it. Simply take those items to your local donation center. You can get a tax receipt and feel good about making sure your items stay out of landfills.

Here are places to donate items:

• Donate items in usable condition to your closest Goodwill or Salvation Army. Some of these companies offer free pickup for large donations.

• Animal shelters will often be happy to take your old linens and towels.

• You can donate craft supplies to schools or local daycare centers.

• You can also donate books to the local libraries.

• Some items such as old newspapers and magazines can be recycled at your local recycling center.

• You can also try posting items for free on freecycle.org or Facebook Marketplace.

DISCARDING YOUR STUFF

Any items that you can't sell or donate are best discarded. Here's the best way to do it.

Recycle what you can. Check with your municipality and take as much as you can to your local recycling center, such as paper, cans, bottles, cardboard, and metal.

Discard what you're allowed. Most trash collectors limit how much garbage you can put out at each pickup. Find out how much you are allowed to put out and make the best use of it.

Hire help if needed. You can also call a junk removal service or a moving company. They will usually take items to be donated if that is your request, but do keep in mind that you may have to pay for these services. (You can use some of the funds from your yard sale!)

ORGANIZING PAPERS, PHOTOS, AND MEMORABILIA

GOING DIGITAL

Everyone has a box, or boxes, of photos and sentimental items. Unfortunately, these are often stored in a shoebox in the basement or attic. This can leave the items vulnerable to heat, cold, humidity, water, or other damage. I recommend scanning fragile papers and photos into a digital format, and then backing them up. (See "Organizing Photos" on page 39 for more on this.) After everything has been scanned and backed up, some people choose to keep the physical photos and papers.

Another benefit to converting your treasures to a digital format is that there is design software widely available to create beautiful custom books and have them printed. You can design scrapbooks or photo albums online yourself or work with a Certified Photo Manager to complete this process.

If you do decide to create a physical scrapbook, you will want to have the pages scanned as a backup when you are finished in case of damage. With this type of project, it is best to give yourself a definite time limit, or else you run the risk of having a project that sits around forever in a half or almost finished state. Don't be afraid to just say "that's enough." Having partially completed craft projects is actually a source of mental clutter, so be careful!

DECLUTTERING SENTIMENTAL ITEMS

Our most sentimental items can be the most difficult to go through and declutter. When going through your most precious items, heed the words of the tidy queen, Marie Kondo, "The best way to choose what to keep and what to throw away is to take each item in one's hand and ask:

'Does this spark joy?' If it does, keep it. If not, dispose of it." This is the simplest and also the most accurate yardstick by which to judge.

One option available is to "camera scan" your most precious items (i.e. take a picture on your phone) and make sure the image is backed up in multiple places. This option is ok, however you will get a better quality scan by using a professional quality camera. With camera scanning you will still have to crop each image individually. You can create a book online with the digital images and add text describing items. Your descendants might not want to take on extra clutter in its physical form, but they may not mind a digital album full of photos and stories about the things that were precious to you. I constantly hear from my clients that their children and grandchildren do not have room in their homes for extra things, and this is a great way to pass on the memories to the next generation.

A good way to put a limit to how many sentimental items you will keep is to select in advance the box in which you will keep these items. Decide how much space you want to devote to these types of things and be strict with yourself. Keep what is truly special in the box and get rid of the rest. My organizer friend Sulena Long calls this a trinkets and treasures chest. She recommends decorating it inside and out so that opening it is exciting and fun.

PARING DOWN PAPER AND MAIL

Find ways to reduce the volume of mail coming in and be sure to allocate regular time to deal with mail. Some ways to reduce the incoming mail are to elect Paperless Billing and Bank Statements, to Opt Out of Credit Card Offers with Equifax (info is included in the fine print of the offer letters), and to limit charitable donations to only a few charities in order to limit request letters. We have some great tips for this in the Chapter on Reducing Paper Clutter With Smart Apps. If you don't have a high capacity shredder in your home, you can take bags of documents to an office supply store and have them shredded (you will usually pay about $1 per pound). If there are a lot of paper files you need to keep, then consider investing in a vertical filing cabinet, which will take up the least amount of space.

Decluttering paper can take time. Be patient and persistent. Stay determined because the benefits of this work are tremendous: A decluttered space leads us to a decluttered mind.

REDUCING PAPER CLUTTER WITH SMART APPS

Is your desk cluttered with papers, greeting cards, important documents, business cards, and more? It probably feels messy, unwelcoming, and overwhelming. With a clean workspace, you offer yourself a highly inviting environment that puts you more at ease in your office. Reducing paper clutter is even more important right now in the aftermath of the COVID-19 pandemic because many more people have been forced, or are choosing to work from their home offices.

As a personal concierge, many of my clients call me because they are overwhelmed by paper clutter. A lot of documents can be thrown out or shredded, but many documents need to be saved, including important and sentimental ones.

There are many ways to organize hard copies of important or sentimental documents, however, I've found that the easiest way is to use apps to digitize them. My favorite apps to help accomplish this are Google Drive, Evernote, and Trello. These apps can help you organize, search for, and quickly find your documents on your smartphone once they have been digitized. Then you can clear your workspace with the confidence that you will be able to find what you need, when you need it.

Here are some ways you can use my favorite three apps to reduce paper clutter in your life. All of these apps have free, basic account options. You can upgrade Evernote and Trello to a paid account if you would like to get more features. Google Drive may charge for storage depending on how much you are storing there. Keep reading for some pro tips on digital organizing and transferring physical paper clutter into digital files.

Google Drive: This is the best way to store documents, PDFs, presentations, and spreadsheets. Google has its own version of Power-Point, Excel, and Word, and these can easily be shared with other users with some practice. You can even use the Google Drive app on your phone so you can share documents with others on the go. I love this feature! I often take notes in meetings, which I put them right into Google Docs to securely save the information with zero paper clutter. The smartphone app for Google Drive also offers camera scanning, which allows you to scan the paper and throw it away. If you only use one app to reduce paper clutter, I recommend this one because it can reduce the greatest amount of paper.

Evernote: As many small business owners know, business cards can quickly multiply when you are attending many different profes-sional networking events. Or as my empty nester clients often complain, you may be struggling with years' worth of greeting cards that are sentimental, but take up a lot of space. How about all those recipes you've been meaning to organize? Evernote is a great way to digitize and organize these types of documents easily, effectively, and with easy searchability. You can camera scan all of these using the Evernote App on your smartphone and then toss the physical business card, holiday greeting card, or cutout magazine recipe. It is organized as a series of "Notes." You assign each Note into a categorized folder (Business Cards, Greeting Cards, Recipes), give it a descriptive title, and add a few details to each Note so it is easily found when needed. In addition to scanning these documents, Evernote also serves as a list-making tool. With this app, you can create lists like Weekly Grocery List and Books I've Read List, all safely organized without creating physical clutter.

Trello: This app consists of a series of boards that you can organize in many different ways according to your needs. You can create a to-do list with Trello cards (each card is a to-do item). It's a great way to remind yourself of things that need to get done at home or work—minus all that paper clutter! One of my father's biggest issues with his to-do lists was losing them all of the time. He would find them much later, at which point he had already crossed off everything on the list. If that sounds like you, Trello is a wonderful solution. It's highly useful for managing home tasks like grocery shopping, yard work, and home improvement projects. It's also ideal for managing work because you can share your boards with other members of your team.

Here are some things you can do with Trello:

- Manage to-do lists
- Set due dates with notifications / reminders
- Share to-dos with other Trello household members and assign them tasks
- Keep long-term projects moving
- Hold other people accountable to completing tasks

Here are a few applications in which Trello could help:

- Create a shared board to help your child keep homework organized.
- Create a board for each child so they can manage their to-dos with your help. (Never again run to the store at 8:55 pm for a poster board.)
- Remind yourself to make dinner reservations and get a gift for a birthday or anniversary.
- Set to repeat each year on a specific date.
- Remind yourself to clean the oven on the weekend.
- In the comments, you could add a link to a how-to article on natural cleaning for ovens.
- Create a repeating to-do for posting onto your business social media weekly.
- Plan out the posts in advance and jot down ideas for yourself in the comments. Add an attachment of another post you liked.

- Plan out large household projects, spring cleaning, or yard sales.
- Add a deadline with notifications and a duplicatable checklist.

What applications would you/do you use Trello for?

Paper Declutter Tip #1: Take 15 minutes before you start tackling your paper clutter to complete a simple organizing plan. The time that you take to create a plan in the beginning will pay back dividends. I use this four-step process.

1. List all the resources you will need, such as a shredder, a binder, and tab dividers for the documents that must have a hard copy saved.

2. List the steps you'll need to take to accomplish the project.

3. Organize those steps into a logical order, from first to last.

4. Write a specific statement about the desired end results you are looking for, such as "I want to be able to find any document within 10 minutes or less," or, "I want my space to make me feel creative and motivated, never stressed."

Paper Declutter Tip #2: Digital filing can be such a wonderful tool if we are able to input specific details to make our documents easily searchable. Here are some things to consider when adding details to your documents to guide searchability.

1. Create separate systems for business and personal files.
2. Use big categories for folders.
3. Sort into alphabetical order.
4. Be specific with file and folder naming. I like to name my files with the date in the first position, so that they will automatically sort by date. A good rule of thumb for file naming is to start on the left with the largest category ex: Household and then move onto the smaller categories ex: Receipts. "2017 Household Receipts would automatically sort below 2017 Household Insurance Policies."

Paper Declutter Tip #3: My organizing class participants are always asking how long to keep papers. The biggest rule of thumb is to keep all tax-related papers for seven years and separate them out into accordion folders, one for each year if you have a business. Personal receipts can usually go into one folder for that tax year, and be sorted out at tax time. Keep warranty and big purchase receipts for as long as you have that item. There's no need to keep clothing or grocery store receipts for more than a few months after you've purchased an item and only keep it if you think you may need to return the item.

Paper Declutter Tip #4: If there is information that is very sensitive or private, digital storage may not always be a good option. There is always a chance with digital storage that your information could be stolen. For this reason, I am always very careful to choose strong passwords and err on the side of caution. With physical information, I choose to shred anything with name and address on it. When it comes to medical information or other very sensitive areas, a physical storage solution may be more secure. Make these decisions based on your individual needs, but make sure you are choosing the systems that work best for you. If you need help researching and making these decisions, I am happy to consult and help you decide on the best solution.

Organizing and reducing paper clutter can help us to simplify our lives. With a clean work or home office desk, we are more productive and at ease in our environment. When our documents are easily searchable, we can find what we are looking for quickly and with much less effort. When we become more organized, we have a greater sense of control over our environment and our lives in general. When we have to waste less time looking for things, we have more time for self-care and can spend more time with our families. Get organized, stress less, be happier, and make the world a better place. Happy digital organizing!

ORGANIZING PHOTOS

Birthdays, holidays, new babies, and weddings: Besides all being gift-giving occasions, these are occasions when we take memorable photographs. For example, looking back at photographs of my best friend at her baby shower and looking at her eight-year-old daughter today, (who now goes to the mall with me), it is very hard to believe that much time has passed.

With more than one trillion photos taken every year, it is more important now than ever to preserve and backup our precious memories properly. As much as we value our physical photos and memories, they deteriorate over time. Physical photos are vulnerable to damage from heat, cold, animals, insects, and mold. Digital photos can be challenging to organize, too. When we take hundreds of photos a year, how do we keep them organized and share them with our friends and family?

When I became a Certified Photo Manager, I learned how to deal with these issues and more. A Certified Photo Manager is a type of professional organizer who works with clients in different areas that have to do with their photo collections. It used to be called A Certified Photo Organizer, however they changed the name to encompass more of the different paths Photo Managers can take. Some Photo Managers focus on scanning and digitizing media, others organize digital image files, and still others create slideshows for families to view together. There are many different avenues, and you can see all of the different services on The Photo Managers Website. Here are some of my top Photo Management tips.

Set a goal. With photo management projects, it is important to define a specific goal before starting. Typical baby boomers have hundreds, if not thousands, of physical photos stored in basements and attics. If you try to do it all in one shot, there will never be an end to your project. It is a better plan to break your project into smaller segments and to work on completing one piece at a time.

One of my first photo management clients gave me several boxes of her family photos and wedding photos to scan, and she defined the specific goal of creating photo albums for her brothers for Christmas gifts. Once we had scanned enough of the photos to create these albums, we sent her draft albums to review before the holiday. We scanned and organized the rest of her photos after the holiday, since this portion of the project was less urgent/time sensitive.

If you grew up somewhere in between paper photos and smartphones, you have the unique challenge of having some digital and some physical photos. If you grew up during the digital age, you likely have all digital photos, but you might have different portions of your photo library stored on different devices. The challenge of organizing all of those images is enough to make your head spin. That is why you should always begin with the end goal in mind.

We all know people who start large projects but quit halfway through. Maybe you have a milestone wedding anniversary or birthday coming up and you want to create an album as a special gift for your loved one. Or, you might be interested in creating a family history document that details the life of a specific family member. Keeping the scope of your project narrow will help you accomplish your goal without getting distracted. Once you complete one goal, you can always start on a new one!

Gather your photos. Photos, photos everywhere! According to Photutorial, 1.2 trillion were taken worldwide in 2021 and 1.72 trillion in 2022. Every year we are taking more and more photos, and it is important to consider where they are stored and backed up. Do you know if your photos are automatically being backed up as they are taken? If not, you might want to find out.

IPhone users have access to ICloud, which is a Cloud Storage platform that backs up photos, videos, contacts and other data stored on your IPhone. Many of my clients are aware of this but do not know how to get the photos out of ICloud. I recommend going onto the website on a computer, signing in with your Apple ID and Password and downloading your photos from there. Once you have them downloaded, you can back them up to either a USB Storage Device or another cloud service in order to achieve the Rule Of 3. We recently worked with a client who wanted us to do this for them, and we downloaded over 10 years worth of photos that had been stored on ICloud. We put them onto 2 External Hard Drives, and a cloud storage platform that they were subscribed to. In addition to their ICloud photos we also converted their DVD's, Mini DVD's, VHS Tapes, Mini DV Tapes, 8mm Tapes, and Photo CD's. Everything was stored in 3 places and there were over 60,000 photos and videos.

Android users have other options available for automatically backing up their photos and videos. One popular option is Google

Photos, which is nice because it offers the ability to organize photos by date or into albums. There are some automation features that can identify the people in your photos based on their tags in other photos, and albums can be created automatically as well. You will have to decide how much you like the convenience, in exchange for Google having the ability to view your photos in order to offer these cool features. According to one of our IT friends they do not guarantee the data, so you will also want to download these photos and make sure that you are still following the Rule of 3 for Backups. Forever Storage also offers automatic backups from your phone with their permanent storage, and there are other similar services available. Choose the best one for your needs based on the price, the features, and the ease of access.

When I started creating a wedding album for my dad for his birthday, I knew that multiple people had taken photos throughout the day. So, I went to Facebook to try to recover them all. Saving all of these photos manually took a lot of time, but once I finished, I knew that I had everything in one place and they were properly backed up. When you go to collect your photos, you may have them on various USB memory sticks, on Facebook, on Apple Photos, and more. This is the time to transfer all of your photos to one place. I tell my clients that the Gold Standard location for your photo library is an External Hard Drive. These are relatively inexpensive compared to what they cost 10 years ago, with 2 Terabytes (enough to store roughly 200,000 photos) being less than $75. So if you purchase 2, with one being the 2nd backup location, you will be two-thirds of the way to the rule of 3! They have the capacity to hold most if not everything that the average person has to store and can plug into a USB port on a computer or even a Smart TV to access the data. They are not as easily misplaced as a small USB Memory Stick, and they will hold everything so you won't have a collection of different Memory Sticks with different sets of photos. When I setup the file structure on these, I usually do them by type of media, so one folder for VHS Tapes, one for 8mm Tapes, etc. For folders with a lot of files, I will also use a date file structure with a folder for each year. How you organize your library will be individual to how you want to access the information, and there are many different ways you can set things up.

I started working with my own digital photos and my goal was to get everything into one place. I put them onto a USB, an external hard drive, and onto the cloud storage platform Forever.com, and I am also keeping the physical photos as a backup. I decided to purchase permanent storage from Forever.com to back my photos up to the cloud and share them with friends and family members easily. It is important to choose a medium that works for your needs when deciding where to save your photo collection. The price of storage on a platform is a major factor for many clients. I decided to go with permanent storage because they offer file converting automatically. I chose to pay a higher lump payment, instead of continuous monthly payments for renting storage.

Digitize paper photos. Any photos that you only have paper copies of should be digitized. You can get them scanned in bulk or little by little, but this is an important step, since having your photos in digital format will allow you to do many more things with them. From printing out albums to setting up a Digital Photo Frame or creating personalized gifts, having your precious photos in digital format opens up a lot of possibilities. It also allows you to store, search for, and view them more easily and you can back them up. You can choose to purchase a photo scanner and do this work yourself at home (warning: it is time consuming), or you can utilize a local Photo Manager. Some local camera shops provide photo scanning services, and there are also services where you ship the photos off to be scanned.

Back them up. It is a rule of thumb that you should save three different copies in two different formats with at least one off-site. In case of fire or flood, this ensures you are not losing something that cannot be replaced. In most cases, your off-site storage will be cloud storage, using Forever.com or another Cloud-based platform. There are many to choose from, and a few that Photo Managers use are Smug-Mug, Amazon Photos, Google Photos, Forever, and Flickr. The benefit to cloud storage is that many of these platforms offer helpful apps that allow you to show off your photos wherever you go. Some offer family shareable albums, which are a great way to keep your photos accessible to others in your family without having to physically mail them copies or take the time to send multiple emails with large photo files.

If you need help, a Certified Photo Manager can gather all of your files in the same place and back them up.

Tag your images. Once you have digitized all of your photos, there are many methods to sort them. One option is to add meta tags to your photos, which are text files attached to a photo file. You can do this by viewing the files in either the Folder or the Finder (depending on whether you use Apple or Windows) and right clicking on the file. You will see options pop up and you will look for either Properties or Info. Once you click on one of those another window will open where you can see the Metadata such as the Date, Description, Etc. This is where you can edit the information and add details. You can use meta tags to add information to your photo such as date, description, location, or people. The date a photo was taken is especially handy. Photos taken with a digital camera or smartphone will automatically include the date and time it was taken. (Of course, that's assuming the date was set correctly.) When you get photos scanned, you can go back and change the dates if you know them. Then you can later sort your photos by date.

Sort your images. Photos can be sorted in many different ways but I generally recommend sorting into folders with the year and month. This is how I am saving my personal photos as I am scanning them. Since my photo envelopes included a gallery photo with the date they were developed, it has so far been easy to identify the month and year. Sometimes old photos were printed with the date and time on the back.

One client worked with me to have her family's collection of slides converted to digital, and the slides were labeled with the month and year they were taken. If your old photos weren't marked with the dates they were taken, sometimes you can make a good estimate based on the age of the photo and the ages of the subjects.

Share your photos. Last but certainly not least, it is time to share your photo treasures with friends and family. The goal of my photo project for my parents' wedding was to create a photo album to give my dad for his birthday. He was really touched because he had not seen many of the photos because they were only in a digital format.

What better activity is there for reunions and special occasions than to pass around a photo album? Or, by giving a print of your great grandparents at their iconic favorite restaurant as a favor? There is no more personal gift than a photo gift, such as a mug, coaster, or holiday ornament. There are so many ways to share photos today. The latest trend is purchasing a WIFI photo frame that allows you to upload photos directly for your loved one, even if they are far away. Some appliances such as smart fridges and security systems allow you to insert a camera memory card and display your photos directly on the screen.

When we are young, everyone is in a hurry to pass the time. We're convinced that what lies in the future is better than what we have. But as we get older, it is a fun hobby to curate and display the beautiful memories that we collect. As we progress into the digital age, we take photos faster than ever before. Unlike the past, now it is easier than ever to make multiple copies of photo files for all of the family members, easier to scrapbook memories, and easier to downsize a collection that takes up almost a full room's worth of space.

Whether you decide to DIY or work with a Certified Photo Manager, the rewards will be immense. You will be able to enjoy the photos that you spend so much time taking and saving. When photos are in an accessible format and backed up for future generations, we can sleep better at night. Our photos are little slices of our lives and they deserve to be preserved and treasured for a lifetime. Looking back on our own past and that of our ancestors can show us who we are and how we got to where we are. Properly stored photos can help with this. What a blessing!

ORGANIZING YOUR MEMORIES

One day, as we stared at shelves full of large totes full of photo memories, my client asked, "Now that I saved all of this, what am I supposed to do with it?"

I replied, "You should keep about 10 percent of what's here, the things that are really special, and put those things in scrapbooks. Get your kids involved and have a good time doing it together."

I made quite a few scrapbooks in my teens and early twenties, and I will be the first to tell you it is a time-consuming labor of love. But when they are finished, it is much easier to flip through a 20- to 30-page scrapbook than hundreds of photos or a zipper lock bag full of random foreign candy wrappers (true story). That is why I am bringing you ideas and tips to get those memory boxes in order—so that you can stop stressing about them and start enjoying them more!

My aunt lives in Florida in the house that my grandmother lived in until she passed away. My aunt asked for my help cleaning out a few cabinets that had been untouched for almost a year since my grandmother's passing. I was honored and happily accepted the project. It was very difficult for my aunt, and she was grateful to have my help.

I begin every organizing project by emptying out the shelves or closet. Then I sort the items, get rid of anything no longer needed, clean the area, and put things back in order. My aunt and I took everything out of the cabinets and placed them onto the kitchen table in categories. Then we went through each category together and decided what to do with each set of items. One set of items was an envelope full of photographs of my great-grandparents, as well as my grandparents in their younger years. I was extremely intrigued because I realized that I didn't know much about many of these ancestors or the lives they had lived. I asked if I could take pictures of the pictures on my phone and my aunt said of course! Back then this was new to me, and I didn't know it's called camera scanning. Later, I called my aunt and she told me who these people were and some of their stories, which I typed up into a document.

I am still working to complete this project, making edits and adding to the stories, but the work I have finished gives me a great sense of connection to my ancestors. Having the document on Google Docs means I can pull it up on my phone. I have sent the document to friends and family, and it gives me a sense of pride to know the stories of my great-grandparents. This type of photo project is just one of the many ways that you can show off your photographs and memories. Keep reading for some more fun ideas!

A few years ago, I had the arduous task of clearing out my family's house. During this project, I stumbled across a bunch of slides and a reel-to-reel video. I decided to invest in a LegacyBox, which is a digitization service for photos and other media. The tough part was deciding which of the slides to send in. After I received my digital files, I had a great time watching a family barbecue from the 1960s. Unfortunately, after a few years I lost the USB that contained the digital files from this project! Fortunately we also received a DVD of these files, and with the help of my local IT firm, we were able to recover the files and back them up properly. When I got them back, I promptly backed the files up in my Forever.com cloud storage account, so that something like this would not happen again.

The family historians on my mother's side of the family were industrious, and they had the idea to document our family history in a typewritten file long before I was born. A few years ago at a reunion, I received a digital file complete with scans of an old family scrapbook. From the scrapbook, I learned about a distant relative who had been a Catholic priest in Allentown and also published a newspaper. A funny story that stuck with me was that one day, he was bringing the typeset trays upstairs and dropped them, making alphabet soup! After this, he gave up on his publishing efforts, and personally I don't blame him.

I have completed a few family history projects for my clients. The Christmas before last, I helped two clients get old VHS tapes digitized. When we received the digital files, I helped one create a video compilation of the home movies. They held a wonderful family viewing party on Christmas Day.

More recently during quarantine, I had a video project for a client's birthday. My client's sister enlisted my help creating a video compilation to make my client's birthday memorable. She gathered video clips from friends and family, and we compiled them into a 10-minute montage of birthday wishes. What a joyful surprise it was for my client during quarantine to see her friends and family and know that were thinking of her.

For photographs, I most frequently preserve them in photo albums. As someone who used to spend hours scrapbooking, I can attest that the photo albums of today are much less time- and space-consuming. When you have your photos scanned into digital format, you can quickly and easily import them into a program that allows you to create a beautiful, professional quality album. If you had to manually glue and paste your photos onto paper, you would be damaging the original, and there is only so much you can do with resizing and filtering. When you make a modern album, you can change the brightness, zoom, and size of your photos in seconds. And a modern album takes up a lot less space because the photos are printed directly onto the paper, instead of having the bulk of the actual photo plus the paper it is attached to, as well as cellulose protectors for each page.

Sometimes, I get ambitious and I create a shadow box from my items. A shadow box is basically a photo frame that has space in between the back and the glass, where you can put items such as wine corks, sports tickets, fabrics, or dried flowers. I created one shadow box for my husband to display his collection of vintage fishing lures and another for his collection of pocketknives. The shadow boxes look wonderful, and it stops the dust from collecting on the items. Being in a shadowbox helps to protect your memory items so that they will last many more years. For a client's baby shower, we purchased a shadowbox for a very special note from a grandparent. Whether you have one item in the box, or many small items, it is fun to look at a shadowbox on the wall. They are a form of bespoke art that adds personality and interest to any room.

Happy memory preserving! The rewards of preserving your memories will pay off for years and years.

ORGANIZING FOR THE HOLIDAYS

With the tools available to us today, it has never been easier to reduce clutter by sending virtual holiday cheer. The pandemic certainly forced us to get a bit creative in order to connect with family and friends. Learning how to connect with far-away family members through video calling technology has been a blessing to families like mine, who are spread across multiple states. Through all of these valuable learning experiences, we have gleaned a few helpful hints on how to get a virtual party started and how to get organized this holiday season to make it feel extra special. Who needs the clutter of party decorations, paper invites, and complicated travel arrangements when you can put together a virtual gathering and celebrate while keeping your environmental impact low?

ORGANIZING YOUR HOLIDAY CARDS

Getting your holiday card list organized and digitizing your old holiday cards can be a great way to Find Freedom from Holiday Clutter. Let's talk about each project in turn.

Creating a Holiday Card List

Before you start this project, I recommend taking 15 minutes to do an organization plan. The time that you take to create a plan in the beginning will pay back dividends.

Before we all had computers and smartphones, people kept old-school lists or address books of family and friends they wanted to mail holiday cards. I inherited my mother's address book, and I love it! Her address book is a three-ring binder with pages I could remove or move as sections filled up.

Today, many of my clients store addresses in their phones.

Pro tip: If you use an iPhone or Google Contacts, you can print out your phone contact lists to make holiday card prep easy and quick.

If you have a large holiday card list, with more than 100 contacts, you will most likely want to use a spreadsheet. If you format your spreadsheet with separate columns for Name, Address Line 1, Line 2, City, State, and Zip in separate columns, you can use mail merge to print labels right from your spreadsheet. You can create labels using Microsoft Word or on Avery.com (my personal favorite). I help clients create these types of labels all the time, so if you don't know how to do this, please feel free to reach out!

Decluttering Holiday Cards

Many times my clients have boxes and boxes of old holiday cards and want to find some freedom from card clutter! If this is you, here's how to accomplish this goal.

Pare down the cards. First, recycle all of the old cards, except the ones that are truly special. If your family is like mine, most of your holiday cards were just signed and did not include a personal message. Only one aunt writes long messages in cards 100 percent of the time. (You know who you are 😊.) So maybe instead of keeping every single card from every single person, you can select one or two cards from each person that are the cream of the crop.

Preserve special messages. If you have cards that you don't need to save that have messages or signatures you do want to keep, here's a compromise: Cut out the message or signature. I have done this, and placed a bunch of the cutouts into a scrapbook, and they fit onto only two pages. I proudly display a message that says "Love, Mom" in a frame with a photo of my mom and me that hangs on my wall. Taking this first step will help save you time and ensure that you are preserving only what is meaningful, instead of putting all of the filler from one format to another.

Digitize old cards. A great way to keep old cards, without taking up tons of space is to digitize them. The tool I use for this is Google Drive. This is an effective tool because you can use the Google Drive App (which comes standard on many phones today) to quickly scan your cards as a PDF, save and share them. Afterwards you can get rid of the physical cards. Just make sure to keep a backup copy of the file on a USB or some other medium, just in case.

Another great app that is similar is Evernote. This tool was designed to help people reduce the amount of physical paper they have to keep. One huge benefit is that written text becomes searchable in Evernote so if you are looking for something but can't remember what you named it, you can search for some of the written text. You can also camera scan your holiday cards using the Evernote App on your smartphone and then toss the holiday greeting card.

If you are not a fan of using apps, you can camera scan your cards or use a printer/scanner. Although this will take longer, when you use the tools that are most comfortable for you, you are more likely to follow through and complete the project.

STORING HOLIDAY DECORATIONS

At the end of December and beginning of January, one of the most popular requests from clients is to pack away the holiday decorations. One of my clients who decorates for every holiday hires me a few times a year to help her store her Valentine's Day, St. Patrick's Day, Easter, summer, and Thanksgiving decorations, too.

Most people love to put decorations up, but not many taking them down. Perhaps putting decorations away signifies the end to all of the joy and magic of the holidays. With all this practice, I have learned some valuable tips to help streamline this process and make it a little bit easier.

Have somewhere to put stuff. One barrier to putting away the decor of the holidays is not having somewhere to put it all. Invest in some large plastic totes for all of your merry gear. They sell inexpensive red and green ones just for this very purpose at stores like Target. If you buy transparent totes, you can tell at a glance what's inside—no label required. One of my clients invested in special divided boxes for ornaments, a circular zip-up bag for her large wreaths, and a Balsam Hill tree that comes with its own special bag for the artificial Christmas tree. When everything has a place, it makes putting things away much easier and quicker.

Pack heavy stuff in the bottom. When you are packing and transporting things, it is very important to keep the heaviest, least breakable stuff in the bottom of the box. For example, if you have brass candle holders or metal stocking hangers, use them to create the very first layer of your packing box. Always remember to keep the delicate, breakable things on the top layer. This principle works in many situations, from the pantry to your suitcase. Remember to pack the largest items first to ensure they will fit.

Tuck in smaller items. After you've put the larger, heavier items into the tote, wrap delicate, smaller items in bubble wrap and place them in the spaces between larger items.

Have boxes inside of boxes. Use shoe boxes or shirt boxes to create some division and organization within your larger totes. For example, a box that once held boots is now the bottom layer of my holiday tote. It is the perfect size and very sturdy, so I don't need to worry about it collapsing.

Save ornament boxes. When you receive a holiday ornament that came in a box, keep the box. These boxes are ideal to store delicate ornaments in because many of them contain inserts that are molded to the actual ornament. As you unpack the holiday stuff, toss the empty boxes back into the empty tote and stuff it into the basement or attic where it was stored. You won't have to worry about breaking your precious Scarlett O'Hara or Hello Kitty and you will have the perfect sized box ready to go when it is time to start packing.

Reward yourself. The hardest part of any project is getting started so give yourself a little reward for starting to put away all of the holiday stuff. Get a milkshake or your favorite Starbucks latte to help keep you going throughout the task. Try enlisting a family member to hold you accountable. A good rule of thumb is to take down the holiday stuff as soon as they start making you feel bad or guilty. If you leave it up too long, it begins to become an energy drain and one more thing you have to do.

Enjoy it while it lasts. The best part about taking down the Christmas stuff is knowing that you had some great times together with family and that another year is in the books. Packing the decorations up can be fun, too. It all depends on your attitude. Try to feel grateful for the holidays, rather than just looking at them as a big annoying chore. I promise, the packing will go a lot faster.

I recently did a survey at an event and found that many people would like to have a "holiday hero" come to take down all of the holiday decorations. This service is provided by a Personal Concierge. If you would rather just outsource this task to a professional, call one of us. You should be relaxing with a glass of wine on your off hours instead of worrying about taking down and packing up all of those decorations.

May your packing be merry and bright!

HELPING OTHER PEOPLE ORGANIZE

Now that you've learned my top tips and you're finding freedom from clutter, your friends and family will take notice, and they might even turn to you for help!

When I started my business and began helping clients organize, I got a few inquiries from my own family. I have had the pleasure of consulting over the phone with one of my uncles who wants to get more organized, helping my father clean out his storage unit, and helping an aunt clear out items after my grandmother passed away.

My family members seemed comfortable asking for help, but it can be really challenging to ask for help organizing. Sometimes people feel embarrassed or worry that they are burdening the other person. Here are some tips to make your family and friends more comfortable asking for your help.

Request something in return. A reciprocal arrangement can help ease the guilt. For example, you could offer the following: I'll be happy to help you organize, if you will make me your famous enchiladas or blueberry pie or buy pizza for lunch while we work! (I guess you can tell that I am very motivated by food!) Just think of something that you can do to help the other person involving your unique skills and offer. Most people will be happy to help if you ask, and a reward at the end will be icing on the cake.

Let them come to you. We all have family members who we wish were more organized. However, if you offer your help in a way that is not kind or is condescending, they are not likely to accept. Think of a way that you can offer your help, and if they accept, great, but it may take them some time. The key to lasting change is that they have to want to get more organized or declutter. If you push someone into it or organize for them without permission, you are likely to damage your relationship and not accomplish anything. Kindly offer your help and if they do not take you up on your offer, just wait. Maybe in the future they will consider making changes.

Set small goals at first. What is the best way to eat an elephant? One bite at a time. And the best way to help someone else get organized is to start small. Set a timer for one to two hours, depending on how long you think the other person can last. Choose the area that is bothering the person most, like her bedroom closet or guest room closet. Take things out and clean the area thoroughly. If the floor hasn't seen daylight in years you will definitely need to vacuum and wipe down the baseboards. Help the other person decide which items she must keep and which can be thrown away or donated. Gauge the person to see if you can push her to get rid of more, or if she needs kid gloves and kind encouragement. Everyone will respond differently, so pay attention to her body language and how she seems to be feeling.

Make sure you take the stuff to sell, donate, or discard. On organizing day, you might persuade your friend or family member to part with some cherished items, but unless you actually remove those items from the home, it's a good bet your loved one will change her mind! Sometimes people will procrastinate with this step, and it's hard to make progress when they can still see all the things they have decided to get rid of around the house. Give them some instant gratification by taking all of their stuff away, never to be seen by them again. Make things easier on the person you are helping by taking her donations to the thrift store.

On your way home, stop by the closest donation center. Don't you procrastinate on this step either. You don't want your car cluttered up with your loved one's things. (For more information on selling, donating, and discarding unneeded items, see "Selling, Donating, and Discarding Your Clutter" on page 28.)

Know when to end the session. Organizing is hard work. It is physically and mentally taxing. Try to keep organizing sessions to three hours maximum, and take frequent breaks for water, coffee, and snacks. This will help you both make better decisions. Try to limit distractions or tangents, which is much easier when you are fully fueled. If you can see that the other person is stressing, or going down the wrong path, call it a day. The last thing you want is for her to get overwhelmed and avoid organizing in the future.

Go at a slow pace and gain momentum. If you let the other person go slowly to start, she will slowly begin to make better decisions. She is asking for your help because she trusts you, and you should be honored.

Ask questions and listen. Sometimes someone will ask you what they should do with a certain item and you may have to use some discretion when telling your opinion. To you it might be obvious trash, but to her it may have some meaning or value. You could ask, "What would you pay for it?" or, "Where could you sell it?" or even, "How long have they been in storage?" Use these types of questions to help the person evaluate the item on her own. That way she is building the skills that will hopefully one day help her organize without your help. A lot of times people will want to tell you stories about items. Try to listen, but also encourage them to leave sentimental stuff until the very end. You can literally open Pandora's box and be there for hours listening to stories, instead of finding stuff to get rid of. Organizing always involves purging – try to do it first and do it often.

Don't organize for them. You are not doing the other person any favors if you just barrel in and do the organizing for her. She learned how to get the stuff. She can certainly learn how to get rid of the stuff. Use the tips above to discourage your need to control the situation. Try to reverse her pattern, and your own, by helping and encouraging, but not taking over the organizing process. Remember, the ultimate goal is for her to organize without you there!

Sometimes you will hit a wall, and notice that the other person has had enough organizing for one day. It can be hard work, not only physically but mentally as well. This is the time to call it a day, clean up, and go grab some lunch or dinner. Spend some time with your loved one and allow her to tell you the stories she was saving about her many treasured items.

If someone you know asks you to help her organize, try to follow these tips so that you will be eating pizza afterward and not screaming at each other. Helping a loved one to organize does not have to be scary. It can be fun and extremely rewarding. Just be prepared to encounter a few dead bugs and cobwebs along the way!

ACKNOWLEDGMENTS

I would like to start off by thanking my wonderful publisher Jennifer Bright. Without all your encouragement and positivity and of course professional prowess, this book would have been an insurmountable task. In the most kind and friendly way possible you followed up with me regularly and checked in with me to find how you could be of help, and this alone helped me more than you know!

I would also like to thank Maria and Scott from the Business Owners Trade Association. Without the power of organization-backed bartering, I would not have been successful in my goal to write a book. During a conversation with Kaitlyn Kozlowski from Kamikoze Tomatoes while we were picking and packing a peck of pickles (something I never would have done if I was not a BOTA member), I told Katilyn I was interested in using my BOTA Dollars to put out a book. And she told Jennifer who contacted me, and my dream became my reality.

I have had many mentors who were themselves authors who inspired me. I would like to thank Tony Mullen, my first client, who was an author who used a book to launch a mission to spread the Flame Of Love. And my second client, Rich Plinke, author of several books, demonstrated the process of inception to publishing for me in real time. He also gave me a push to cross the finish line and held me accountable to doing the work. Another friend and author Danielle MacKay inspired me with her simple message that she put into her children's book. Also, Rita Guthrie for demonstrating how becoming an author can help your business, and inspiring me to continue going on with my book as I read the stories of the Local Luminaries that she helped bring to life.

Also, I would like to thank my wonderful team members who had a hand in helping me with this book. Thank you to Kelly Henriques and Tom Harper for helping me put my ideas into words that became blogs that were the starting point for some of these chapters. And thank you to Val Garcia, Mary O'Brien, Lynn Warrington-Dirga, Damla Alkan, and Sharon Grant for helping me move the book forward by editing the manuscript. I appreciate all of the work that you all contributed that made this book possible.

And thank you to every client that I've had the pleasure of organizing for. I have appreciated the opportunity to come into your homes/businesses and make them a better place. Thank you for your trust in me and my abilities. It has been an honor to serve you all. I especially would like to thank C. Mullen, V. Wischhusen, G. Alkan, S. Rhodes, S. Bostian, and H. Leon for projects that taught me invaluable skills and were the basis for some of the stories used in this book.

I would most definitely like to thank my wonderful husband, John O'Brien, for all of your support and encouragement throughout this process. The eternal realist, my sounding board and my coach— without you on board I would have never taken the steps to make this book happen. I appreciate all of your love and your belief in me.

Of course I would like to thank my father, Paul Warrington, for taking care of my little baby while I worked on finishing the book. And for helping me craft the section on Organizing for Other People. And for setting an example with your writing. I can not wait to read the book that you are working on about how you survived the sinking of FV Liberty. It will be an epic sea tale!

And thank you to my sweet baby, Maggie, for giving me a purpose that is so much greater than anything I've ever had before. I promise to set an example that will allow you to be Free from Clutter all of your days. You are my shining star and I love you with all of my heart.

Lastly, I would like to thank my mother, Carolyn Draving, for trusting me with the duty of being her will executor which set me on a path that led me to help others Find Freedom from Clutter. I will always remember you and love you. I wish you could have been here to see what I have accomplished in your name and meet your darling little granddaughter, Maggie.

If there is anyone that I have not mentioned specifically, I sincerely thank you for your contribution to this work and appreciate all that you have done!

ABOUT THE AUTHOR

Melissa Draving is a Personal Concierge, Professional Organizer, and Certified Photo Manager who lives in Emmaus, Pennsylvania. She started her business Here For You Concierge in 2017 to help others have more time to give back to their families, by helping with things they don't know how to do, don't have time for, and/or normally procrastinate. As one client beautifully put it "You help others do things they have wanted to do for a long time." She has worked with over 100 clients, some on a weekly basis and others just for projects. In 2021 she learned about Photo Management and decided to become certified after helping several clients with their photo projects.

Melissa grew up in lovely Doylestown. Her mother was the owner of a recorded music store, and she worked there from a young age, first helping vacuum for quarters and later as a key-holding 16-year-old cashier. Her mother Carolyn was an inspiring female business owner and breadwinner. Melissa has one half brother who is older and lives in California. When Melissa was in her early twenties she went to Germany to become an au pair. 2017 was her "Big Year" during which she got married to her husband, John O'Brien, started her business, and moved to Emmaus, where she and John bought their first home, and also adopted their beagle, Annie.

During the process of writing this book Melissa and John welcomed their daughter, Maggie, into the world and adopted a puppy named Hank. They love walking around town with the stroller and of course Annie and Hank too. Her other hobbies include cooking, trying new restaurants and coffee shops, taking ballet classes, doing puzzles, and shopping.

Melissa loves to inspire others, and in writing this book she hopes that others will be inspired to do the same thing. Her motto is Zig Ziglar's quote "If they can do that, I can do a whole lot more!" And she hopes you will follow her example and work on your own masterpiece. As Zig Ziglar also says "Start where you are, with what you've got, and you can get anything that you want."

ABOUT HERE FOR YOU CONCIERGE

Making your life easier ✓

- hereforyoupa.com
- https://www.facebook.com/HereForYouConcierge
- https://www.instagram.com/hereforyouconcierge/
- https://www.linkedin.com/in/melissadraving/

Services Provided:

- Professional Organizing
- Personal Assistance
- Personal Shopping

- Errand Running
- Photo Management